HELLO

MY NAME IS:

My birthday

My signature

Published by Collins
An imprint of HarperCollins Publishers
Westerhill Road
Bishopbriggs
Glasgow G64 2QT
www.harpercollins.co.uk

HarperCollins Publishers
1st Floor, Watermarque Building, Ringsend Road, Dublin 4, Ireland

First edition 2020

10 9 8 7 6 5 4 3 2

© HarperCollins Publishers 2020

ISBN 978-0-00-837260-6

A catalogue record for this book is available from the British Library

ACKNOWLEDGEMENTS
Publisher: Michelle l'Anson
Concept creator: Fiona McGlade
Author and Illustrator: Kia Marie Hunt
Project Manager: Robin Scrimgeour
Designer: Kevin Robbins
Photos © Shutterstock

Special thanks to the children at Golcar Junior Infant and Nursery School

Printed by GPS Group, Slovenia

MIX
Paper from
responsible sources
FSC™ C007454

This book is produced from independently certified
FSC™ paper to ensure responsible forest management.

For more information visit: www.harpercollins.co.uk/green

My AWESOME Year Being

6

Written and illustrated by
Kia Marie Hunt

Contents

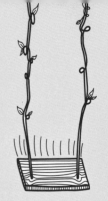

Hello!

Your year being 6 is going to be AWESOME
now that you have this book to record it in!

You're about to discover SO MANY fun
activities, projects, recipes, and other
exciting new things to try...

Start by writing your name, birthday,
and signature just inside the front cover.

Near the end of the book, there are blank
pages where you can continue with any
of the activities, try something again,
or just do whatever you like!

Just inside the back cover, you can draw
or write about a fun thing you did for each
month of your awesome year being 6!

P.S. You might need a grown-up's help to do some of the things
in this book, so ask them to read the note on page 128.

~~Rules~~

1. Do the activities in this book in any order you like.

2. You could use pencils, pens, highlighters, crayons or paints to answer the questions. Feel free to make a mess!

3. Why not colour in the drawings?

4. Why not add your own doodles?

5. You can write your answers, draw, or even stick photos in. Do it your own way!

6. HAVE FUN and remember that you are awesome!

All about me

What do you look like?

(Draw yourself.)

Where do you live?

What are you good at?

What is awesome about you?

Who gave you this book?

(Remember to say thank you to them.
They are fantastic!)

9

A **day** in my life

This page is all about your day!

What are the first 3 things you do when you wake up each morning?

1 ....

2 ....

3 ....

What is your favourite part of the day and why?

....

....

....

....

What do you like to eat for...

Lunch?

Breakfast?

Your evening meal?

Draw or write in the shapes.

What are the last 3 things you do before going to sleep?

1 ....

2 ....

3 ....

My amazing **family**

How many people are in your family?...........

List their names:

. . . .

. . . .

Draw your family here:

Don't forget to include yourself!

What is the best thing about your family?

. . . .

. . . .

. . . .

What is the best thing your
family do together?

. . . .

. . . .

. . . .

5 things I liked about being 5

What were the 5 best things about being a 5-year-old? Write or draw one thing inside each balloon.

7 things I want to do before I am 7

Think of 7 things you want to do before you are 7. Perhaps you'd like to try something you've never done before, or want to visit somewhere new?

You don't have to do this all in one go. You can add some things then come back to it later.

Write them down and tick each one off when you've done it.

1 .... ☐

2 .... ☐

3 .... ☐

4 .... ☐

5 .... ☐

6 .... ☐

7 .... ☐

My **super senses**

What is your favourite sound?

_____

What is the worst sound ever?

_____

 What do you think is the most
beautiful thing to look at?

_____

What is the ugliest sight you've ever seen?

_____

What is your favourite smell?

_____

What is the worst smell ever?

_____

What is your favourite flavour?

_____

What is the most disgusting flavour ever?

_____

What is your favourite thing to touch?
How does it feel?

_____

_____

What feels horrible to touch? Why?

_____

_____

My favourite **song**

What is the name of your favourite song?

_____

Who sings it?

_____

What's your favourite line in the song?

_____

_____

_____

How does this song make you feel?

Sharing **songs**

Ask a friend or someone in your family what their favourite song is and then listen to it together.

Who did you ask?

What was their favourite song?

Who sings it?

Did you like it?

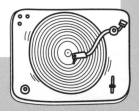

Life **outside**

Do you often spend time outside?

When you play outside, where do you go?

Who do you spend time outside with?

What is your favourite activity to do outside?

When it's sunny outside I like to...

When it's raining outside I like to....

When it's snowing outside I like to...

Nature's **superhero**

What do you love most about nature?

_____

Draw your favourite thing in nature.

If trees could
talk, what do
you think they
would say?

Nature needs you!

If you were a superhero with a mission to help nature, what would your costume look like?

Draw it here and complete what your superhero is saying.

My nature-saving power is

I will protect

Nature hunt

Grab a backpack, some snacks, drinks, and your walking boots, because it's time for a nature walk...

Date:

Where are you?

Write your answer.

Can you find a colourful rock?

Draw it here.

2 Can you find a strange insect? ☐

Draw it or stick in a photo, if you're quick enough to take one!

3 Can you find leaves in the colour of traffic lights? One red leaf, one orange or yellow leaf, and one green leaf! ☐

Draw or stick them to the page.

4 Can you find something that has an interesting texture? ☐

Draw what you found.

How does it feel?

5 Can you find a tiny flower? ☐

Draw or stick in a photo.

6 Can you find a bird? ☐

7 Can you write your name in sticks and twigs? ☐

If you ticked off all 7 items, well done! You just completed your nature hunt.

Recipe: Easy-peasy banana blender **pancakes**

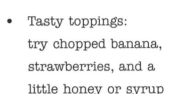

Ingredients

- 2 ripe bananas
- 2 eggs
- 2 tablespoons of self-raising flour
- 1 teaspoon of baking powder

- Tasty toppings: try chopped banana, strawberries, and a little honey or syrup

How to make

1. Peel the bananas and break them into a few pieces.
2. Crack the eggs and put them into the blender.
3. Add the flour, baking powder, and bananas to the blender too.
4. Whizz the ingredients together until you have a smooth batter.
5. Add a little butter to a frying pan on a low-medium heat.
6. Pour a little puddle of batter into the pan and cook for a minute.
7. Flip your pancake over and cook on the other side.
8. Serve your pancake and add some tasty toppings.

REMEMBER!
Safety is important, so don't try this on your own!

What did you enjoy most about
making this recipe?

_____

_____

What tasty toppings
did you add?

Draw your pancakes:

_____

_____

_____

_____

How did they taste?

Rate
this recipe
out of 5

1=Yuck!
5=Yum!

 **I ♡ school**

What is your school called?

_____

What year are you in?

_____

Who is your teacher?

_____

What is your favourite subject? Why?

_____

_____

What is your least-favourite subject?

_____

What is the best thing about going to school?

_____

_____

_____

What is the worst thing about going to school?

_____

_____

If you could make one new school rule, what
would it be and why?

_____

_____

_____

MY
HOMEWORK

My fantastic **friends**

Who are your friends?

List their names and write down what you like about them.

Name of friend	What I like about them

What do you like to do with your friends?

_____

_____

Who is your best
friend and why?

Draw your best friend
or stick a photo here:

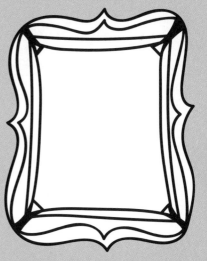

_____

_____

_____

_____

What is your favourite memory
with your best friend?

You can
write or
draw.

I'm **happy** when...

What are 3 things that make you smile?

You can write or draw.

Draw a place that makes you feel happy.

My favourite **book**

What is your favourite book?

What is the book about?

Who is your favourite character?

What is your favourite part of the story?

How does the book make you feel?

Being a 6-year-old
bookworm

Every time you read a book that you like,
write the title below.

Visiting a **farm**

Take a trip to a farm and see what you can find...

Date: _____

What was the name of the farm you went to?

_____

Who did you go to the farm with?

_____

What did the farm look like?

Draw or stick in a photo.

Which animals did you see?

Write the names of the farmyard animals you discover below (or draw what they look like) and count how many you see!

What was your favourite thing about visiting the farm?

_____

_____

My dream
birthday party

Imagine the best birthday party EVER!

Where would it be? Describe the place:

. . . .

. . . .

Who would you invite? Write your guestlist:

. . . .

. . . .

What activities would you do?

. . . .

. . . .

Draw what you would have to eat and drink:

Don't forget the cake!

What awesome presents might you get?

....

....

....

My **hobbies**

Do you have any hobbies? _____

What is your favourite hobby?

(Or your favourite way to spend your free time.)

Write, draw, or stick in photos.

What other things do you like to do after school and at the weekend?

Write, draw, or stick in photos.

What new hobbies would you like to try?

_____

_____

Sing sing **sing!**

How does singing make you feel?

Where do you think is the best place to sing?

(In your room where no one is listening? In the playground?
In front of an audience? When you're in the bath?!)

_____

Write down the name of a song that is really
fun to sing out loud...

_____

Your challenge is to make up a new song.
You could sing it to yourself, sing it to a
friend, or sing it to your family!

Date: _____

What is the name of the song you made?

_____

How would you describe it?

_____

Who did you sing it to?

_____

_____

Where did your performance take place?

_____

Did you enjoy it?

My **holiday**

Think of a holiday or special trip you have been on recently.

Where did you go?

When did you go?

How did you get there?

Who did you go with?

What was your favourite part of the holiday or trip? Why?

- -

- -

- -

Do you have any photos from your holiday or trip? Stick one here.

(Or you could draw the place you visited instead.)

Sports superstar

What sports do you do?

Which sport are you best at?

Do you think being good
at sport is important?

Why or why not?

How does playing sports make you feel?

Sports day

Have you ever taken part in a sports day?

Where was it?

When was it?

What did you like the most about taking part in a sports day? Why?

FINISH

My favourite **sport**

What is your favourite sport?

_____

Why is it your favourite?

_____

_____

Rate how *well* you think you can play your favourite sport:

1 = I'm rubbish – but I love it anyway!

2 = I'm still learning...

3 = I'm quite good

4 = I'm very good

5 = I'm an expert!

Rating out of 5

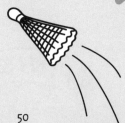

Where do you usually play your favourite sport?

_____

_____

Who do you usually play it with?

_____

_____

_____

If you could be amazing at any sport, which one would it be?

_____

_____

_____

What makes me **laugh**

How often do you laugh?

Only sometimes ☐
Every day ☐
All the time! ☐

KNOCK, KNOCK!

WHO'S THERE?

Write down something that makes you laugh.

(It could be a book, film, TV programme, or on the computer.)

_____

What is the funniest joke you have EVER heard?

_____

_____

_____

_____

Who is the funniest person you know?

_____

How do they make you laugh?

_____

Do you think you are a funny person? _____
Why or why not?

_____

_____

Describe how it feels to make
someone else laugh.

_____

_____

_____

Recipe: Rainbow fruit kebabs with delicious dip

Ingredients

- Red fruit like strawberries, raspberries, or watermelon.
- Orange fruit like mango, peaches or, of course, oranges!
- Yellow fruit like pineapple or bananas.
- Green fruit like kiwi or green grapes.

- Blue and purple fruits like blueberries, red grapes, or blackberries.
- 2 cupfuls of yoghurt (plain or flavoured)
- **Optional extras**
  - 1 tablespoon of honey
  - Half a teaspoon of ground cinnamon
  - A few mint leaves

How to make

1. Ask a grown-up to help you prepare your colourful fruit. Some of the bigger fruits will need to be chopped into chunks.

REMEMBER! Safety is important, so don't try this on your own!

2. Carefully add your fruit onto long thin kebab skewers piece-by-piece.
3. Try to include every colour of the rainbow in each kebab. (You can add them in rainbow order or mix it up a bit!)
4. Put your yoghurt in a small bowl with any extras like honey, cinnamon or mint. Stir it all together, this is your delicious dip!

Which colourful fruits did you use?

_____

_____

How did they taste?

Draw or stick in a photo of
what your kebabs looked like:

Rate
this recipe
out of 5

1=Yuck!
5=Yum!

Being a 6-year-old
parkrunner

A parkrun is where you get to run around a
park with lots of other people.

Junior parkruns are for children aged 4 to 14,
so you will be very welcome!

1. Ask a grown-up to help you go to the website **parkrun.com**
   to sign up and find a junior parkrun near you.
2. On the day, make sure you wear some comfy running clothes
   and running shoes.
3. You can choose to run fast, jog, walk, or even hop, skip or
   jump around the course if you want to!

No matter how you take part,
you'll definitely have lots of fun
joining in with a parkrun.

Write about your experience
on the next page.

Date: _____

Where did you do your parkrun?

_____

_____

What was your running number?

_____

How far did you run?

_____

How long did it take you?

_____

Did you enjoy it?

_____

Visiting a place of **worship**

Visit a place of worship that you've never been to before. It could be a church, gurdwara, mandir, mosque, synagogue, temple...

Date: _____

What place of worship did you visit?

_____

Who did you go with?

_____

What was the best thing about your visit?

_____

Draw something you liked from the outside
of the building (or stick a photo here):

Draw something you liked from the inside
of the building (or stick a photo here):

My **good deeds** diary

Being kind is fun, free, and feels good.

Your challenge as a very kind 6-year-old is to do lots of good deeds and write them down in your 'good deeds diary'.

Date	My good deed

Date	My good deed

My favourite **film**

What is your favourite film?

_____

How many times have you watched this film?

_____

What is your favourite part of the film?

_____

_____

_____

How does watching this film make you feel?

Sharing **films**

Ask a friend or someone in your family what their favourite film is and watch it together.

Who did you ask?

What was their favourite film?

Did you like it? Yes ☐ No ☐

Why or why not?

Collecting **textures**

1. Collect some materials that have different textures.
   Here are some ideas:
   - Something **rough** (like sandpaper)
   - Something **shiny** (like tin foil)
   - Something **fluffy** (like cotton wool)
   - Something **soft** (like velvety fabric)
   - Something **crinkly** (like a sweet wrapper)

2. On a piece of plain paper, draw a picture with big open shapes
   that you can fill in with different textures. Why not try a
   hedgehog in a field, like this?

3. Rip or cut your materials into different shapes and stick
   them onto the paper to fill out parts of your drawing.

4. Well done, you just made a collage out of your
   texture collection!

When you have finished your collage, run your hands across it. Which texture do you like the best? Why?

_____

_____

Stick in a photo of what your collage looks like (or draw it) here:

Did you enjoy making your collage? _____

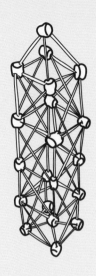

Building the tallest **tower**

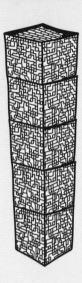

Build the tallest tower you possibly can!

You could build your tower out of anything you want: building blocks, boxes, crayons, or even marshmallows!

Ask a grown-up to help you build the tower out of something that won't hurt you if it falls.

(Grown-ups are also great for helping out when the tower gets too tall!)

Tip: Have a tower-building competition with a friend or family member to see who can build the tallest tower!

Date: _____

What did you build your tower out of?

_____

How tall was it? _____

Draw your tower or stick in a photo:

Did you have fun building it? _____

Keep on **moving!**

Circle which exercise you like best out of...

 Running
or walking

 Jumping jacks
or skipping

 Dancing **or**
hula hooping

 Hurdles **or**
hopscotch

What is your favourite exercise?

Where do you like to do your favourite exercise?

How often do you do it?

Are you good at it?

How does exercising make you feel?

😦 😮 🙂 😅 🥰 🤩

Set **sail**

Make a boat and see if it floats!

What you'll need

- 8 corks
- The plastic lid from a tub of butter or margarine
- Some PVA glue
- Scissors
- A straw
- A hole punch
- Sticky tape
- 2 pieces of paper
- A small toy person or animal to sail your boat!

How to make

1. Cut 1 piece of paper into a rectangle that covers your plastic lid. Use PVA glue to stick it to the lid.

2. Cut the other piece of paper into a triangle.

3. Use the hole punch to make a hole at the top of the triangle and a hole at the bottom. Put the straw through the holes, this is your sail!

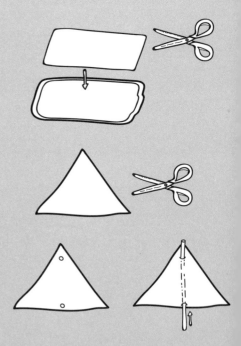

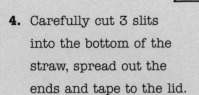

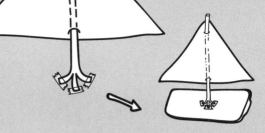

4. Carefully cut 3 slits into the bottom of the straw, spread out the ends and tape to the lid.

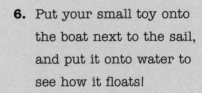

5. Glue all of the corks to the other side of the lid.

6. Put your small toy onto the boat next to the sail, and put it onto water to see how it floats!

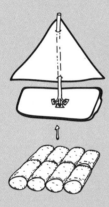

Did your boat float well? _ _ _ _ _ _ _ _ _ _ _ _ _ _ _

What was the best thing about making your own boat?

_ _

_ _

_ _

Left-handed or **right**-handed?

Are you left-handed ☐ or right-handed ☐?

Write your name with the hand you usually write with:

_____

Write your name with the other hand:

_____

Draw a doodle with the hand you don't normally use!

Now, try to do one of these other things but with the hand you don't normally use:

- Brushing your teeth
- Opening the lid of a bottle
- Pouring a drink
- Eating (switch your knife and fork!)
- Playing an instrument

What did you do?

_____

_____

Was it difficult or easy?

_____

_____

Did you enjoy these activities?

The **Throw and Catch** Olympics

What you will need

- A small ball or a soft mini beanbag for throwing
- A hula hoop
- A bench or box that is safe to stand on
- A friend or family member to be your competitor!
- Some bowling skittles (or empty plastic bottles)

Game 1

- Put your hoop on the ground and stand in the middle of it.
- The other person has to stand back and throw the ball or beanbag into your hoop.
- If you catch it, you get the point.
- If it lands inside your hoop, they get the point!
- Then swap.

Game 2

- Stand up on a safe bench, box, or step.
- The other person has 5 turns to throw the ball or bean bag up to you while you're balancing.
- For every one you catch, you get a point!
- Then swap.

Game 3

- Stand 9 bowling skittles (or bottles) in a triangle shape on the ground.
- Take it in turns to throw your ball or beanbag and knock down as many as you can.
- You get a point for each one you knock over.
- Stand them all up again after each try.

Date:

Who did you play the Throw and Catch Olympics with?

Which game did you like the best?

How many points did you get?

Who won?

Face-painting

Face-painting is a fun activity whether you're going to a birthday party or just want something to do on a rainy day!

You can try painting your own face, or you could paint a friend or family member's face and ask them to paint yours.

Ask a grown-up to help you find some skin-friendly face paint (or make-up).

Here are some design ideas

- Your favourite superhero
- Rainbows, flowers, and butterflies
- A tiger, lion, or cat
- Another amazing animal of your choice!
- Something spooky like a skeleton, zombie, or witch (great for Halloween!)

Date: _____

Whose face did you paint?

_____

Draw your face-painting design
or stick a photo of it here:

Did you enjoy face-painting?

How does your
garden grow?

Starting your own mini herb garden is easy and fun!

1. Ask a grown-up to help you prepare a container like a window box (or a few pots) with some good soil for growing things.
2. Plant some seeds for the herbs you want to grow. Here are some great ideas for fast-growing, nice-smelling, tasty herbs:
   - Basil – pop it on your pizzas!
   - Mint – chop and add to lemonade!
   - Chives – add to anything cheesy!
   - Rosemary – delicious with roast potatoes!
   - Coriander – great in curries!
   - Rocket – add to salads for a peppery flavour!
3. Put your herb garden somewhere sunny. Water it every other day (in summer) or whenever the soil gets dry (in winter).
4. Keep checking your herbs as some of them will grow much faster than others!
5. When your garden has grown, cut some and use them to add extra flavour to your food.

Date you planted your herb garden:

_____

What herbs did you put in your garden?

_____

Date you saw the first plant begin to grow:

_____

When your herb garden has grown, draw what it looks like or stick in some photos here:

Recipe: Tasty tomato **soup**

Ingredients

- 2 tins of chopped tomatoes
- 1 garlic clove
- 1 small onion
- 2 tablespoons of tomato purée
- 2 tablespoons of olive oil
- 450ml of vegetable stock
- Bread and butter
- A handful of herbs like basil, chives or rosemary (grow your own, see page 78!)

How to make

1. Ask a grown-up to help you chop the garlic and onion, open the tins, and put the saucepan onto a medium heat.
2. Put the olive oil in the saucepan. After a minute, put in the chopped onion and garlic.
3. After about 5 minutes, put the tomato purée and tinned tomatoes in too. Mix it all together.
4. After a few minutes, put in the stock bit-by-bit, stirring as you go.
5. Add in your handful of herbs and let them simmer in your soup on a low heat, until hot.
6. Then serve up the soup with some buttery, crusty bread.

REMEMBER!
Safety is important, so don't try this on your own!

What did you enjoy most
about making this recipe?

_____

_____

How did it taste?

Rate
this recipe
out of 5.

1=Yuck!
5=Yum!

Stick in a photo of what your
soup looks like, on top of this
one, if you want!

Making a **secret club**

Keep this book
somewhere safe,
because you're
about to start a
super secret club!

Shhhhh!

Only tell the
grown-up who is
helping you with
this page!

Write down a name for your secret club.

- -

Draw a logo for your club.

Write down a secret password that only the people in your club will know:

Where will your secret meeting place be?

Who will you invite to join your club?

(If you want, you can give each person in your club an awesome title like **The Club Captain**, **The Secret Spy**, **The Meeting Master**, **The Snack Supplier**...)

What will you do in your club?

(Will it be a club where you secretly make or do something together? Maybe there's a problem you need to solve? Or a mystery you want to investigate?)

What are the top 3 rules of your club?

1 ....

2 ....

3 ....

Date of your first meeting:

‗ ‗

What did you do or talk about?

‗ ‗

‗ ‗

‗ ‗

‗ ‗

Riding my bike

Can you ride a bike? _____

Do you think learning to ride a bike is easy?

_____

Draw your bike:

(If you don't have one, draw your dream bike!)

Where is the best place to ride a bike?

(Write or draw your answer.)

Who would be the best person to go on a bike ride with?

_____

_____

When I **grow up**...

Fill in the gaps.

When I grow up I want to be...

_____

_____

_____

because... _____

_____

I will live in... _____

_____

with... _____

_____

Draw the outfit (or uniform) you think you will wear when you are a grown-up:

What do you think will be the best thing about being a grown-up?

_____

_____

Furry friends

Do you have any pets? _ _ _ _ _ _ _ _ _ _ _ _ _ _ _ _ _ _ _

If yes, what pets do you have and what are their names?

_ _

_ _

If no, what pet would you like to have, and what would you call it?

_ _

_ _

What do you think is (or would be) the best thing about having a pet?

_ _

What do you think is (or would be) the worst thing about having a pet?

Draw your pet (or your dream pet!):

Let's go **pond-dipping!**

You're about to become a 6-year-old pond-dipper! Let's find out all about pond-life...

What to wear

- Old clothes that keep you warm enough and that you don't mind getting a bit wet
- Waterproof plasters to cover any cuts or scratches you might have
- Your wellies!

BE SAFE!

Make sure you always go pond-dipping with a grown-up, never alone!

What to take

- A net with a long handle (for catching)
- A light-coloured tray or other shallow container (for looking at what you find)
- A magnifying glass (to get a closer look!)
- A camera (if you have one)
- A towel (for drying your hands)
- Spare dry clothes and socks (just in case!)
- A plastic bag (to keep this book dry)
- This book and some pens (for drawing)

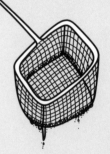

What to do

1. Walk to the pond slowly and quietly so you don't scare anything away.

2. Ask a grown-up to help you add some pond water to your tray or container. This gets it ready for the creatures you might find!

3. Dip your net into the water and slowly glide it around in the shape of an 8.

4. Carefully empty whatever's in your net into your tray. Take care as some of the creatures you find might be tiny!

5. Have a good look at what you have found, using your magnifying glass to look closer.

6. Take photos of any interesting creatures (or draw them on the next page).

7. Gently empty your creatures back into the pond and try again in another part of the pond!

Note: Make sure your net is washed properly once you are finished in the pond, especially if you are going to another pond after.

Write about pond-dipping on the next page.

Date: _____

Where did you go pond dipping?

_____

_____

Who did you go with?

_____

_____

What did you find in the pond?

_____

_____

_____

_____

Draw or stick in a photo of your favourite
pond creature:

What was the best thing about going
pond-dipping?

_____

_____

_____

My dream **bedroom**

Design the room of your dreams!

What would you have on the walls?

(A colour? Patterned wallpaper? Something else?)

What would your bed look like?

(Triple bunk beds? A water bed? A hammock?)

How would you get into your room?

(A secret tunnel? A slide? A zip line?
Pick any cool entrance!)

Choose one more fun thing to add...

(A tree? A swing? A swimming pool? It could be anything!)

A trip to the **park**

It's time to explore another new place.
Visit a park you've never been to before!

Date: _____

What park did you go to?

Go with a grown-up, don't explore a new park on your own!

_____

_____

Who did you go with?

_____

What was the best thing about this park?

_____

_____

Draw what the park looked like, and what you did there (or stick in a photo):

Did you enjoy your visit?

My favourite game

What is your favourite game?

_____

_____

What is the game about?

_____

_____

Where do you like to play it?

_____

Who do you like to play it with?

_____

Sharing **games**

Ask a friend or someone in your family what their favourite game is and play it together.

Who did you ask?

What was their favourite game?

Did you like it? Why or why not?

My toys

What are your 4 favourite toys?

(Write about them or draw them.)

Where do you keep your toys?

_____

_____

If you could talk to one of your toys,
which one would you talk to?

_____

_____

If you could have any toy in the world,
what toy would you have?

_____

_____

Lava lamp experiment

What you will need

- 3 half-litre plastic bottles (cleaned)
- A funnel
- Water
- Vegetable oil
- Food colouring
- Table salt
- A black marker
- Glitter and sequins (optional)
- A torch (optional)

Get a grown-up to help you with this experiment!

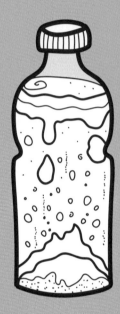

What to do

1. Use your marker to write a number on each bottle: 1, 2 and 3.
2. In a jug, mix together some water and a few drops of food colouring.
3. Pour the colourful water into bottle 1 until it is a quarter full.
4. Pour the colourful water into bottle 2 until it is half full.
5. Don't put any water into bottle 3 yet! Pour vegetable oil into this bottle until it is two-thirds full.

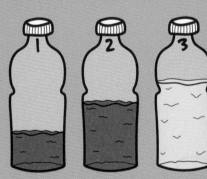

6. Fill the rest of bottle 1 and bottle 2 with vegetable oil (leave a small gap at the top).

7. Fill the rest of bottle 3 with colourful water (leave a small gap at the top).

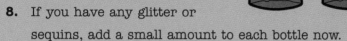

8. If you have any glitter or sequins, add a small amount to each bottle now.

9. Get ready for the fun part! Add a large spoonful of salt into each bottle.

10. Make sure you put the lids on tight. Now watch the show!

Tip: Turn the lights off and shine the torch into each bottle to see the lava lamps even better!

Results

Date: _____

Who did you do the lava lamp experiment with?

_____

Did you enjoy the experiment? Yes ☐ No ☐

What was your favourite part?

_____

Turn the page...

Which lava lamp was better: 1, 2 or 3?

_____

Draw what your lava lamps looked like
or stick in a photo:

The Science Bit

Salt is heavier than oil and water.

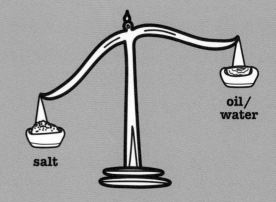

oil/
water

salt

As the salt sinks, it pushes some of the oil to the bottom of the bottle.

As the salt dissolves, the oil is no longer trapped beneath the salt and can rise up through the water.

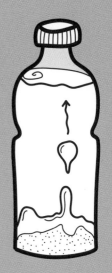

My **wishes**

If you had 3 magic wishes,
what would you wish for?

It can't
be 'more
wishes',
that's
cheating!

Have you ever had a wish come true?

Yes ☐   No ☐

If yes, what was it? How did it come true?

If no, do you think one of your wishes will come true one day?

My favourite **outfit**

What is your favourite outfit?

Draw it or stick in a photo.

Why is it your favourite?

(Do you like the colours? The pattern? How it feels?)

_____

_____

_____

Fashion designer

Design an awesome outfit. You can draw
or stick bits of material to the page!

Family are **friends** too!

Choose a member of your family
who you think is also a good friend.

(It could be a brother, sister, cousin,
aunt, uncle, grandparent, or someone else.)

What is their name? _____

How are they related to you? _____

What do they look like?

Draw
them or
stick in
a photo.

What is awesome about them?

_____

_____

What is your favourite thing to do together?

Write, draw, or stick in a photo.

Ask this family member to write a message to you here:

_____

_____

Picking **fruit**
and **vegetables**

Along with a grown-up, visit somewhere where you can pick fruit or vegetables.

(It could be a strawberry farm, a pumpkin patch, an allotment, or even just a field where you can pick blackberries.)

Date: _____

Where did you go? _____

What did it look like?

Draw it or stick in a photo.

Who did you go with?

_____

Which fruit or vegetables did you pick?

Draw and label them.

What was your favourite part of the day?

_____

_____

Being a 6-year-old **poet**

Write a poem about something you've done in this book. It can be long or short, serious or silly, you can choose!

Here are some rhyming words to give you ideas...

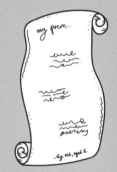

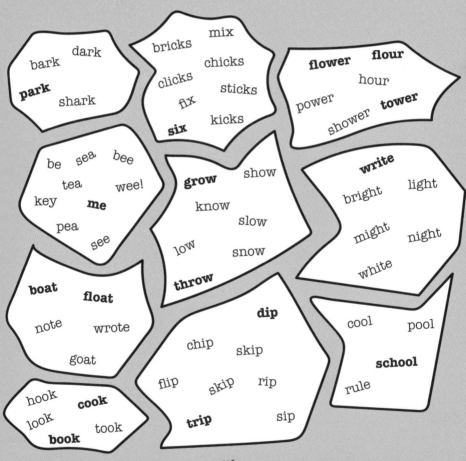

bark   dark
park
shark

bricks   mix
chicks
clicks   sticks
fix
six   kicks

flower   **flour**
hour
power
shower   **tower**

be   sea   bee
tea   wee!
key   **me**
pea
see

grow   show
know
slow
low   snow
throw

write
bright   light
might   night
white

boat
float
note   wrote
goat

dip
chip   skip
flip   skip   rip
trip   sip

cool   pool
school
rule

hook   **cook**
look   took
book

116

Write your poem here:

_____

_____

_____

_____

_____

_____

_____

_____

_____

You can continue it on the next page if you want!

My awesome year being 6

You
can write,
draw, or
stick things
in!

A note to grown-ups

You can join in the fun too by sharing experiences together, discussing the activities and celebrating accomplishments throughout the year! And remember to help with some of the recipes and other tricky tasks.

Follow us on Instagram @Collins4Parents where we'll be hosting regular competitions and giveaways as well as giving you extra ideas to make the year **even more awesome!** Share your experiences with the book using the hashtag #MyAwesomeYearBeing

My Awesome Year series

9780008372606   9780008372613

9780008372620   9780008372637   9780008372644

My year of **fun**

January	February

March	April

May	June